BRILLIANT BRITS

DAVID

BECKHAM

RICHARD BRASSEY

Orion
Children's Books

Who is the most famous footballer in the world today?

Who turned up for a trial at Tottenham wearing a Man U kit?

Who scored the longest goal in competition history?

Who runs further than any other Man U player in every game?

DAVID BECKHAM

David Robert Joseph Beckham was born on 2 May 1975. He grew up and went to school in Chingford, Essex. His dad Ted is a gas engineer. His mother Sandra is a hairdresser. He has an older sister, Lynne, who hates football, and a younger sister, Joanne, who loves it.

Ted had always wanted to be a professional footballer. As soon as David could walk, he encouraged him to kick a ball about. Although they lived in East London, Ted supported Manchester United. Every Christmas he gave David a new United strip.

When d'you think he'll start walking?

But David's granddad on his mum's side supported nearby Tottenham Hotspur. Every Christmas he gave David a new Spurs strip. Ted was terrified David might grow up to be a Spurs supporter, but David never had any doubts. It was always Man U for him.

David was always kicking a ball around the garden. He ruined all the flowers. Every day after school he raced to the park and stayed long after his friends had gone home. He'd play "keepy-uppy" for hours on end.

Often his dad helped him practise and they'd stay out until 11 pm. Sometimes his mum used to get worried. The only time David ever stopped practising was to watch his dad play Sunday league or to watch football on TV.

When he was seven David answered an ad in the local paper and was chosen to play for the Ridgeway Rovers, a local boys' team. The coach immediately recognised David's skills, but he had some doubts. Although you wouldn't think it now, David was very small and skinny for his age.

WANTED
Football superstars of the future. Only talented boys need apply.
Box 416

He's got legs like a canary!

He's a good striker but he's very weedy!

Wait till you see his dead-ball skills.

The Rovers were easily the best team in their league. For three years they won every game. During his time with them David played 115 games and scored an amazing 101 goals. His dead-ball skills were outstanding. Even at that age he could put a corner right into the goalmouth!

Then one day he saw a bit on Blue Peter about Bobby Charlton's Soccer Schools. He entered and got through to the final, which was held right on the pitch at Old Trafford, the Man U ground! Not only that – he came top, with the highest score ever. Sir Bobby said he was the best eleven-year-old he'd seen.

His prize was to fly to Spain and train for two weeks with the Barcelona youth team.

You need to practise, practise and keep practising.

At that time Terry Venables was the Barca coach and Gary Lineker was the main striker. Mr Venables told David to practise as much as he could.

When he got back, David was invited on a TV show to demonstrate his skills.

This is David from Essex.

But normal life had to go on. To earn pocket money David got a job collecting dirty glasses at Walthamstow Greyhound Stadium.

Good job you had a good game. A scout from Man U is coming round to see us!

He was very disappointed when he was told he was too small for the England Schoolboys team. But he played for the Essex Boys. After one match his mum had some amazing news. A scout from Man U had been watching.

David was fourteen when he signed schoolboy forms with Man U. For the next two years he spent all his holidays training at the club. Soon after his sixteenth birthday manager Alex Ferguson signed him on as a youth trainee.

Apart from practising their skills, trainees had to do all sorts of jobs like cleaning seniors' boots and sweeping the floor.

One of the other trainees was Gary Neville, who became David's best friend. There was also Gary's brother Phil, Nicky Butt, Paul Scholes and Ryan Giggs. It's not surprising the youth team won the FA Youth Cup in 1992!

That's my son!

That same year David made his first team debut against Second Division Brighton. But it would be another two years before he made the first team again . . . and scored his first goal for Man U. His dad leapt right out of his seat with excitement!

Mr Ferguson was worried that David was not strong enough at winning the ball. He loaned him to Third Division Preston North End for some first team experience. In his first game for Preston David scored from a corner. After only five games Mr Ferguson wanted him back.

David played his first Premiership match against Leeds in April 1995. The following season he played in thirty games. It was a great season. Man U topped the Premiership and won the FA cup at Wembley.

At the start of that season David did something truly amazing when Man U played Wimbledon. He picked up the ball in his own half and sent it sailing right down the pitch over the keeper's head into the goal . . . from 57 yards. Nobody had ever scored such a long goal in competition history.

David's brilliant goal was no accident. He practises shots a hundred times over. Sometimes he does it barefoot. He says it helps him to feel the ball.

He is always training. He comes in on his days off and goes to bed early.

When he started at Man U he was only 5'4". But he trained with weights and ate sensibly. Now he's 6 feet tall.

Four years in a row David was Essex County 1500 metre champion. He's been measured as running 8.8 miles per game, further than any other Man U player.

In 1996 David had been made captain of the England Under 21s. Later that year Glenn Hoddle, the England manager, called him up for the first squad.

The 1996/7 season was a good one for David. He was voted Man U Young Player of the Year . . . and won the Sir Matt Busby Award.

When Man U striker Eric Cantona retired, David inherited the No 7 shirt which had once been worn by his hero, Bryan Robson, and the legendary George Best (David is No 7 in the England team, too).

And he met 'Posh Spice' Victoria Adams, who was one of the Spice Girls – the most successful pop group in the world at that time.

When David first met Victoria he was so shy he just said "Hi!". They met again and got talking, and this time Victoria gave David her number. He was so worried he might lose it that as soon as he got home he wrote it down on seven different pieces of paper. The next day he drove to London to take her out.

Victoria took him to meet Melanie C, one of the other Spice Girls. Mel had Liverpool posters on the wall. But they got on really well and soon he'd met all the Spice Girls. When the newspapers found out, it was big news. Early the next year David proposed to Victoria. She was so surprised she asked him to do it again.

David was in for a big disappointment when World Cup '98 began in France. The manager left him on the bench. But in the second match against Romania Paul Ince was injured. David came on, to loud cheers from the England supporters.

You're not focused enough, David.

This is the most disappointing moment of my entire career.

Then 18-year-old Michael Owen came on and scored the first of his wonder goals for England. England lost the game, but the supporters had seen enough. They wanted David and Michael in the team.

They had to beat Columbia in the next match to go through. David made sure of it by putting a great free kick in the net.

David would never forget the next match, against Argentina. The Argentine captain, Simeone, had been tugging his shirt and trying to put him off. Then he sent David crashing with a tackle from behind. As he lay on the ground David lifted his foot and tripped Simeone.

If David ever argues with the referee, his grandma tells him off. She watches all his matches on TV and she can lipread!

Simeone got a yellow card for the tackle, but David was sent off. He admits that as soon as he was off the pitch he burst into tears. England struggled on into extra time with ten players, but they were beaten on penalties.

It seemed as if the whole country blamed David for England's defeat. Even the manager spoke out against him.

It cost us the game.

BOO!

10 HEROIC LIONS. ONE STUPID BOY!

BOO!

BOO!

Beckham's silly little kick

I want every England supporter to know how deeply sorry I am.

BOO!

BOO!

Wherever he played people booed him. Instead of letting it upset him, David apologised. He went on to play some of the best football of his career.

It was United's best season ever. They won the Premiership, the FA Cup and the European Cup. In March 1999 David set up both goals to beat Simeone's club, Inter Milan. At the end of the game he made a point of swapping shirts with Simeone.

The very next day something even better happened. Victoria gave birth to a son, Brooklyn. She had told David she was going to have a baby when he flew to be with her after he was sent off in the Argentina game. They were staying in a part of New York called Brooklyn.

David has always made it clear that his family is the most important part of his life. In July he and Victoria had a grand wedding at a castle in Ireland. They both had thrones to sit on. Gary Neville was best man.

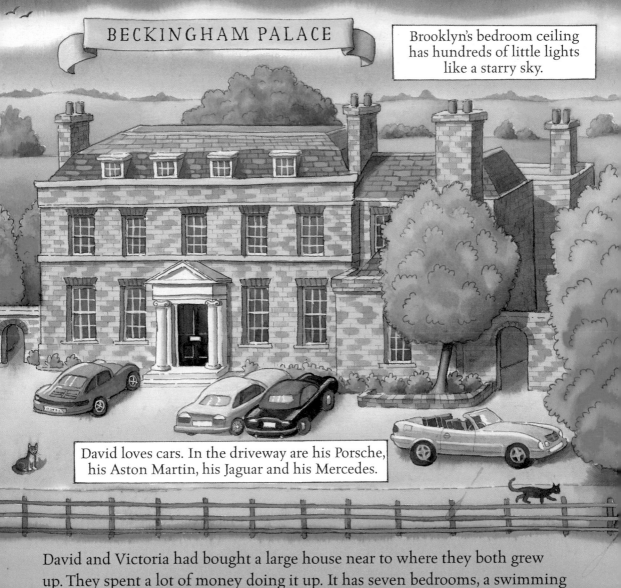

BECKINGHAM PALACE

Brooklyn's bedroom ceiling has hundreds of little lights like a starry sky.

David loves cars. In the driveway are his Porsche, his Aston Martin, his Jaguar and his Mercedes.

David and Victoria had bought a large house near to where they both grew up. They spent a lot of money doing it up. It has seven bedrooms, a swimming pool, a snooker room, a gym, and tennis courts. The newspapers thought it was so grand they immediately nicknamed it Beckingham Palace.

David has always loved clothes. When he was seven he had to be a pageboy at a wedding. His mother was worried people might think he looked silly, but he thought he looked really smart.

Once he famously wore a sarong, which is rather like a skirt. He has far more clothes than Victoria and he folds them up. Victoria is rather untidy.

I'm comfortable in it.

David has several tattoos. On his back is a guardian angel to look after his family. Brooklyn's name is tattooed beneath it.

Although it hurts, he plans to have all his children's names tattooed under the angel . . . So he can't have too many children or there won't be enough room on his back!

BROOKLYN

David is always changing his hairstyle. Below are some styles he's tried . . .

. . . and some he hasn't tried yet. You can make up the last one!

But David and Victoria don't spend all their time at the hairdresser's. They lead very busy lives. Something they try to do often is visit children who are in hospital. What a nice surprise to wake up and find David and Victoria sitting by your bed!

As England set out to qualify for World Cup 2000, a mood of hope gripped the fans. David Beckham was to be captain and a confident new coach had been appointed – Sven Goran Eriksson.

England won five matches in a row, but in the final qualifier against Greece they seemed to go to pieces. It was the captain who saved the day. He was everywhere at once. Seconds before the final whistle, he scored with a free kick. England were through!

Then disaster ... two months before the finals, David fractured a bone in his left foot during a Champions' League match. Would it heal in time for the World Cup?

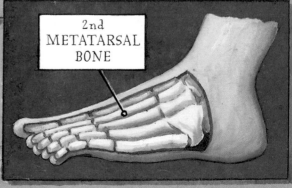

2nd
METATARSAL
BONE

Two months later . . . huge relief! The fracture had healed. The captain was on his way to Japan. But although he had done his best in the gym, he'd been out of the game and was not 100% fit. Despite this, England got through their group . . . and they beat Argentina! David scored the winning goal with a trademark penalty. And after the game he shook Simeone's hand.

David coolly prepares to take the penalty against Argentina. The whole world is watching on TV.

The ball travels at nearly 100 mph!

Unfortunately Beckham's men were knocked out 1-2 in the quarter finals by the eventual winners – mighty Brazil. But they'll be back!

In any case David had plenty to be happy about. Second son Romeo was born two months later.

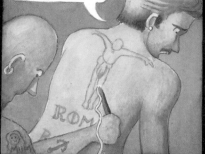

One thing is certain. We have not seen the last of David Beckham. And when eventually he retires from football, he has another ambition . . . to go to the moon. He won't have any trouble breaking his own 57 yard record with only the moon's gravity!